*Communities at Work*™

# Community Needs

## *Meeting Needs and Wants in Communities*

**Jake Miller**

The Rosen Publishing Group's
## PowerKids Press™
New York

Published in 2005 by The Rosen Publishing Group, Inc.
29 East 21st Street, New York, NY 10010

First Edition

Editor: Natashya Wilson
Book Design: Maria E. Melendez
Layout Design: Albert B. Hanner

Photo Credits: Cover and pp.1, 5, 13 © Ariel Skelley/Corbis; p. 7 © Don Mason/Corbis; p. 9 © Todd A. Gipstein/Corbis; p. 11 © Royalty-Free/Digital Vision; p. 15 © Royalty-Free/Digital Stock; p. 17 © Tom Stewart/Corbis; p. 19 © Michael Keller/Corbis; p. 21 © Kelley-Mooney Photography/Corbis

Library of Congress Cataloging-in-Publication Data

Miller, Jake, 1969–
Community needs : meeting needs and wants in communities / Jake Miller.
     v. cm. — (Communities at work)
Includes bibliographical references and index.
Contents: Community needs and wants — Community needs — Community wants — Food to eat — Clean, fresh water — A place to call home — Making and doing — Keeping the community safe — Community leaders — Coming together.
ISBN 1-4042-2780-6 (lib. bdg.) — ISBN 1-4042-5012-3 (pbk.)
1.  Human services—Juvenile literature. 2.  Basic needs—Juvenile literature. 3.  Community life—Juvenile literature.
[1. Human services. 2. Basic needs. 3. Community life.] I. Title. II. Series.

HV31.M47 2005
361—dc22

2003027584

Manufactured in the United States of America

# Contents

# Community Needs and Wants

People who live and work together form a **community**. Cities, towns, and families are examples of communities. In a community, people help one another get the things that they need and want. Needs are things that people must have to **survive**. Wants are things that people enjoy.

*People in a community need food to eat. They need a water supply, such as a lake. The people may want a park. Parks are places where community members can gather and have fun.* ▷

# COMMUNITY NEWS

The kinds of things that people need can change. Years ago, people needed hay to feed their horses. Today they need gas for their cars.

# Community Needs

The first thing a community must do is to make sure that people have the things they need to stay alive. Nobody can live for long without things such as healthy food and clean water. People also need a safe, clean home. They need warm clothes during cold weather. When people work together in a community, it is easier for people to get what they need.

*Grocery stores are places where people buy food and other things that they need. Almost every community has one or more grocery stores.* ▷

# Community Wants

After everyone's needs are met, people in a community can work together to get things that they want. They can build a **library** or a community center. They can hold a town fair. They can make music and art. People like to live in a community that helps them to get things that they want.

*People visit Ellis Island because they want to learn about the history of their families.* ▷

# Making and Doing

The people in a community have many different jobs. Some people make **goods**. Other people supply **services**.

People need and want all kinds of goods and services. When people make goods or supply services, they are called **producers**. When people buy goods and services, they are called **consumers**.

*This worker is fixing a part in a factory. He is supplying a service.* ▷

## COMMUNITY NEWS

People need certain foods. They need vegetables. They need foods that have protein, such as meat. People do not need desserts. Desserts are a want.

## Food to Eat

People need food to stay alive. They want to eat food that tastes good. Communities can get food in many ways. In a farm community, people can grow their own crops. They may raise or hunt animals for food. People in town and city communities may not have room to grow their own food. They buy food in stores.

*A family shares a meal. Food is a need. It is also something that can bring a community together.* ▷

13

# Fresh, Clean Water

Everyone needs clean water to drink. Water also fills many other kinds of needs and wants.

For example, farmers need water to grow crops. Firefighters need water to put out fires. People need water in their houses to do things such as taking baths and washing dishes. They may want water for a swimming pool.

*Farmers need a lot of water to grow crops. If the place they live in does not get enough rain, they may also need big sprinklers for watering the crops.* ▷

# A Place to Call Home

All people need a place to live. Different places have different types of homes.

In the country, people may live far away from their closest neighbor. In a city, one building may have more than one hundred **apartments**. In a town or a **suburb**, many people have houses that are close to their neighbors' houses.

*In a town or a suburb, many people live in houses. They may live close to their next-door neighbors. Houses in towns and suburbs often have front yards and backyards with trees in them.* ▷

# Keeping the Community Safe

People want to live in a safe community. Communities need people to help keep the community safe. For example, firefighters put out fires to stop people from getting hurt. Police officers make sure that people do not break the law. Parents take care of children. Doctors and nurses work to stop illnesses.

*When people get sick or hurt, doctors help to make them better. Sometimes people do not want to go to the doctor, but they still need to go!*

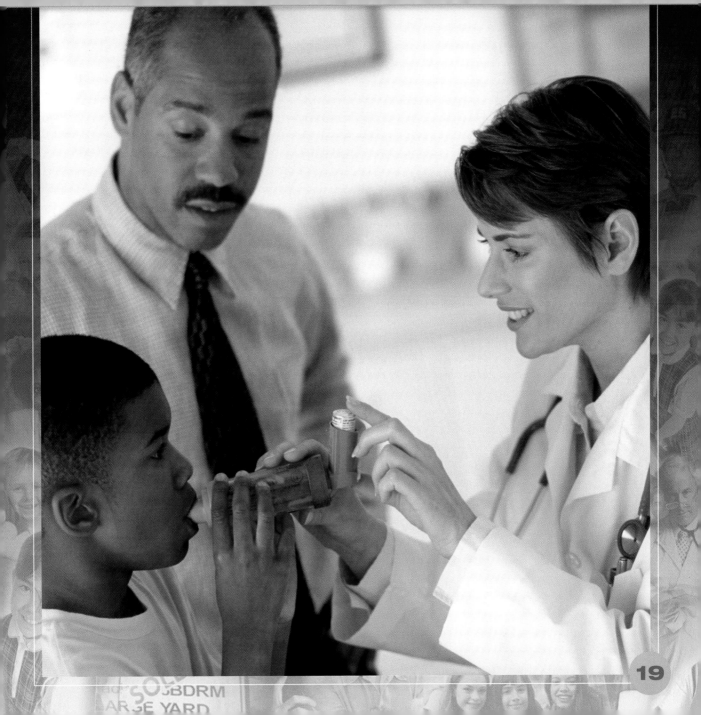

19

# Community Leaders

In a community, there are many different people. They all have different needs and wants. People choose leaders to keep track of all the needs and wants. A town or city has a **mayor**. A school has a **principal**. Leaders and community members work together to make sure that everyone is treated fairly.

*Chicago mayor Richard M. Daley marches in a parade that honors the city's Greek community. The mayor of a city tries to help all the different people that make up the community.* ▷

# Coming Together

In a community, people work together to get the things that they need and want. They build homes and grow food for one another. They keep each other safe. They meet one another on the street, in shops, and in the park. They share more than just a place. They share their lives.

# Glossary

**apartments** (uh-PART-ments)  Sets of rooms that a family lives in that are in a building with many other sets of rooms and families.

**community** (kuh-MYOO-nih-tee)  A place where people live and work together, or the people who make up such a place.

**consumers** (kun-SOO-merz)  People who buy things.

**goods** (GUDZ)  Things that people can buy and sell.

**library** (LY-brer-ee)  A place that stores books, magazines, and videos that people in a community may borrow.

**mayor** (MAY-ur)  The leader of a town or a city.

**principal** (PRIN-sih-pul)  The leader of a school.

**producers** (pruh-DOO-serz)  People who grow or make things that will be sold.

**services** (SIR-vis-ez)  Things that people do for other people.

**suburb** (SUH-berb)  An area of homes and businesses that is near a large city.

**survive** (ser-VYV)  To stay alive.

# Index

**C**
city(ies), 4, 12,
    16, 20
consumers, 10
crops, 12, 14

**F**
food, 6, 12, 22

**G**
goods, 10

**H**
home(s), 6, 16,
    22

**J**
jobs, 10

**L**
library, 8

**M**
mayor, 20

**N**
needs, 4, 8, 14,
    20

**P**
police officers, 18

producers, 10

**S**
services, 10
suburb, 16

**T**
town(s), 4, 12,
    16, 20

**W**
wants, 4, 14, 20
water, 6, 14

# Web Sites

Due to the changing nature of Internet links, PowerKids Press has developed an online list of Web sites related to the subject of this book. This site is updated regularly. Please use this link to access the list:

www.powerkidslinks.com/caw/comneeds/

24